manifest your dreams

2024

WEEKLY PLANNER

JULY 2023–DECEMBER 2024

ROCK
POINT

2024 Year at a Glance

JANUARY

S	M	T	W	T	F	S
	1	2	3	4	5	6
7	8	9	10	11	12	13
14	15	16	17	18	19	20
21	22	23	24	25	26	27
28	29	30	31			

FEBRUARY

S	M	T	W	T	F	S
				1	2	3
4	5	6	7	8	9	10
11	12	13	14	15	16	17
18	19	20	21	22	23	24
25	26	27	28	29		

MARCH

S	M	T	W	T	F	S
					1	2
3	4	5	6	7	8	9
10	11	12	13	14	15	16
17	18	19	20	21	22	23
24	25	26	27	28	29	30
31						

APRIL

S	M	T	W	T	F	S
	1	2	3	4	5	6
7	8	9	10	11	12	13
14	15	16	17	18	19	20
21	22	23	24	25	26	27
28	29	30				

MAY

S	M	T	W	T	F	S
			1	2	3	4
5	6	7	8	9	10	11
12	13	14	15	16	17	18
19	20	21	22	23	24	25
26	27	28	29	30	31	

JUNE

S	M	T	W	T	F	S
						1
2	3	4	5	6	7	8
9	10	11	12	13	14	15
16	17	18	19	20	21	22
23	24	25	26	27	28	29
30						

JULY

S	M	T	W	T	F	S
	1	2	3	4	5	6
7	8	9	10	11	12	13
14	15	16	17	18	19	20
21	22	23	24	25	26	27
28	29	30	31			

AUGUST

S	M	T	W	T	F	S
				1	2	3
4	5	6	7	8	9	10
11	12	13	14	15	16	17
18	19	20	21	22	23	24
25	26	27	28	29	30	31

SEPTEMBER

S	M	T	W	T	F	S
1	2	3	4	5	6	7
8	9	10	11	12	13	14
15	16	17	18	19	20	21
22	23	24	25	26	27	28
29	30					

OCTOBER

S	M	T	W	T	F	S
		1	2	3	4	5
6	7	8	9	10	11	12
13	14	15	16	17	18	19
20	21	22	23	24	25	26
27	28	29	30	31		

NOVEMBER

S	M	T	W	T	F	S
					1	2
3	4	5	6	7	8	9
10	11	12	13	14	15	16
17	18	19	20	21	22	23
24	25	26	27	28	29	30

DECEMBER

S	M	T	W	T	F	S
1	2	3	4	5	6	7
8	9	10	11	12	13	14
15	16	17	18	19	20	21
22	23	24	25	26	27	28
29	30	31				

2025 Year at a Glance

JANUARY

S	M	T	W	T	F	S
			1	2	3	4
5	6	7	8	9	10	11
12	13	14	15	16	17	18
19	20	21	22	23	24	25
26	27	28	29	30	31	

FEBRUARY

S	M	T	W	T	F	S
						1
2	3	4	5	6	7	8
9	10	11	12	13	14	15
16	17	18	19	20	21	22
23	24	25	26	27	28	

MARCH

S	M	T	W	T	F	S
						1
2	3	4	5	6	7	8
9	10	11	12	13	14	15
16	17	18	19	20	21	22
23	24	25	26	27	28	29
30	31					

APRIL

S	M	T	W	T	F	S
		1	2	3	4	5
6	7	8	9	10	11	12
13	14	15	16	17	18	19
20	21	22	23	24	25	26
27	28	29	30			

MAY

S	M	T	W	T	F	S
				1	2	3
4	5	6	7	8	9	10
11	12	13	14	15	16	17
18	19	20	21	22	23	24
25	26	27	28	29	30	31

JUNE

S	M	T	W	T	F	S
1	2	3	4	5	6	7
8	9	10	11	12	13	14
15	16	17	18	19	20	21
22	23	24	25	26	27	28
29	30					

JULY

S	M	T	W	T	F	S
		1	2	3	4	5
6	7	8	9	10	11	12
13	14	15	16	17	18	19
20	21	22	23	24	25	26
27	28	29	30	31		

AUGUST

S	M	T	W	T	F	S
					1	2
3	4	5	6	7	8	9
10	11	12	13	14	15	16
17	18	19	20	21	22	23
24	25	26	27	28	29	30
31						

SEPTEMBER

S	M	T	W	T	F	S
	1	2	3	4	5	6
7	8	9	10	11	12	13
14	15	16	17	18	19	20
21	22	23	24	25	26	27
28	29	30				

OCTOBER

S	M	T	W	T	F	S
			1	2	3	4
5	6	7	8	9	10	11
12	13	14	15	16	17	18
19	20	21	22	23	24	25
26	27	28	29	30	31	

NOVEMBER

S	M	T	W	T	F	S
						1
2	3	4	5	6	7	8
9	10	11	12	13	14	15
16	17	18	19	20	21	22
23	24	25	26	27	28	29
30						

DECEMBER

S	M	T	W	T	F	S
	1	2	3	4	5	6
7	8	9	10	11	12	13
14	15	16	17	18	19	20
21	22	23	24	25	26	27
28	29	30	31			

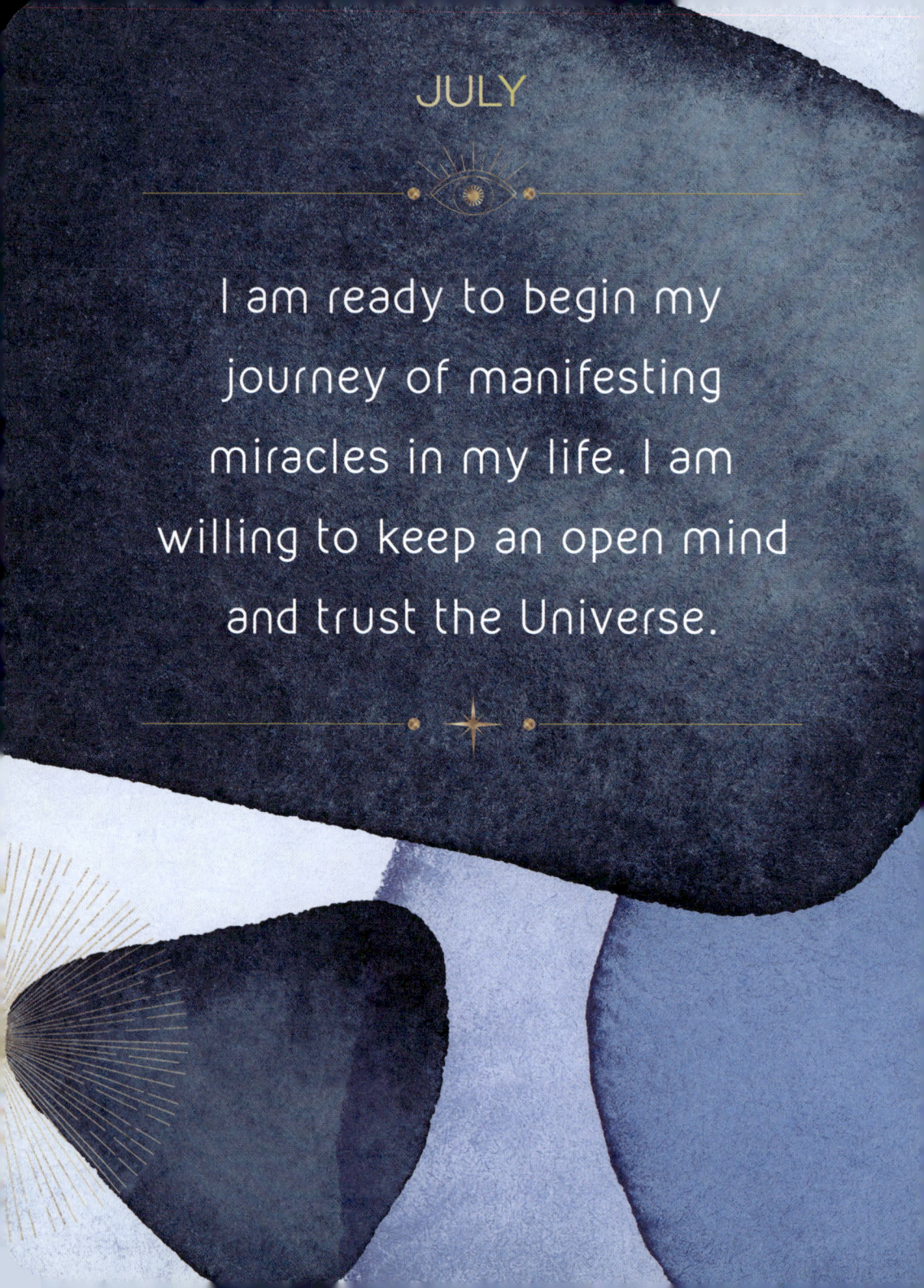

JULY

I am ready to begin my journey of manifesting miracles in my life. I am willing to keep an open mind and trust the Universe.

MANIFESTING YOUR DREAMS

You have the gift of free will. No one else is responsible for creating your reality. You alone control your thoughts, feelings, and vibration. It is within you, not any external person or circumstance. You are in the driver's seat. Are you ready to take your life off autopilot and start truly living a life of fulfillment?

Let's break down the manifesting process:

1. Get crystal clear on what you desire.
2. Bring awareness to the limiting beliefs that say you can't have it or you are unworthy of it.
3. Replace limiting beliefs with positive affirmations and certainty.
4. Take inspired action.
5. Hold the vision, be patient, and continue having unwavering faith until it manifests.

July 2023

	SUNDAY	MONDAY	TUESDAY
	2 ○	3	4
			INDEPENDENCE DAY (US)
	9 ◗	10	11
	16 ●	17	18
	23	24 ◖	25
	30	31	

July 2023

WEDNESDAY	THURSDAY	FRIDAY	SATURDAY
			1
			CANADA DAY (CAN)
5	6	7	8
12	13	14	15
19	20	21	22
26	27	28	29

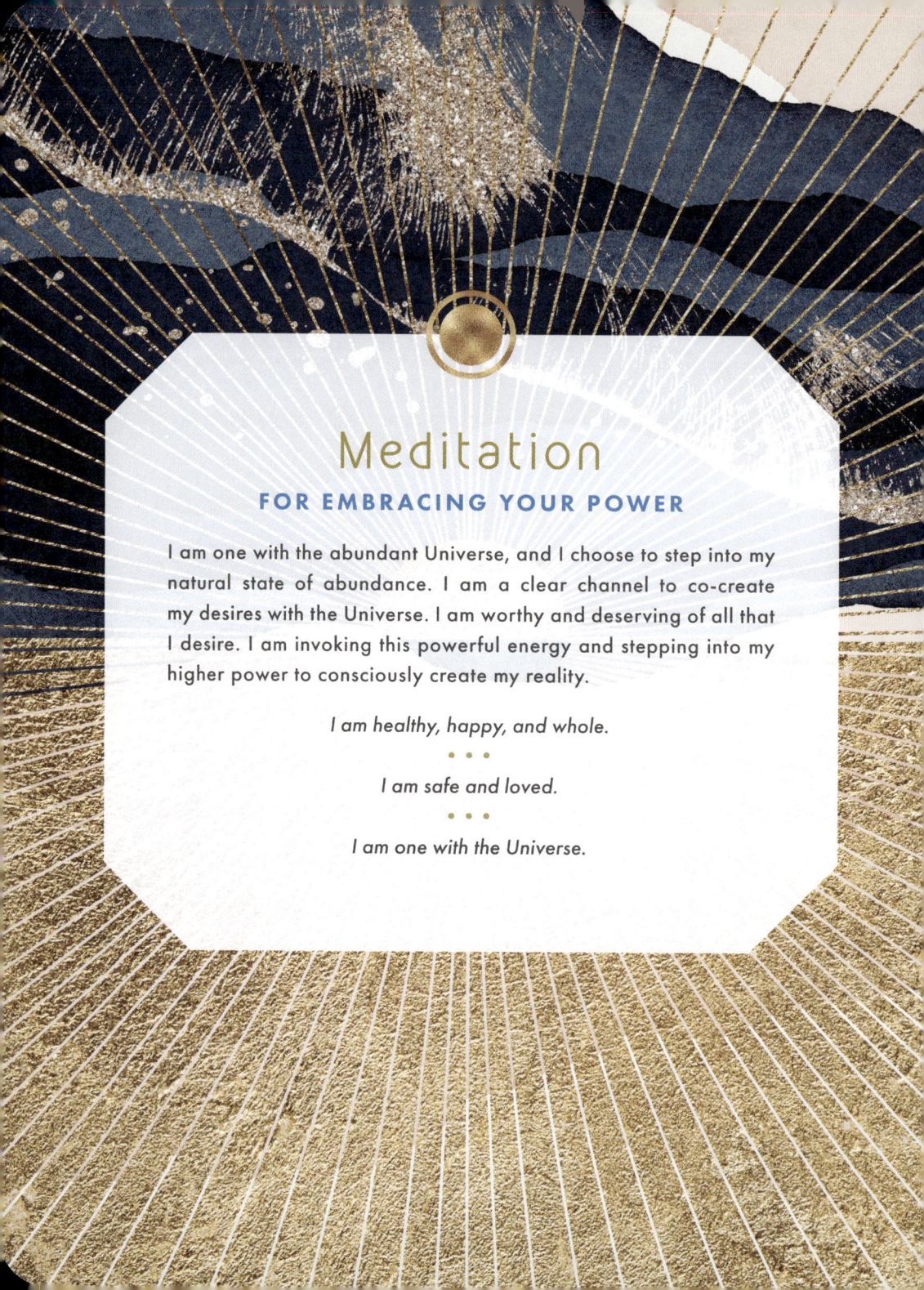

Meditation

FOR EMBRACING YOUR POWER

I am one with the abundant Universe, and I choose to step into my natural state of abundance. I am a clear channel to co-create my desires with the Universe. I am worthy and deserving of all that I desire. I am invoking this powerful energy and stepping into my higher power to consciously create my reality.

I am healthy, happy, and whole.

• • •

I am safe and loved.

• • •

I am one with the Universe.

June/July

MONDAY (JUNE)	26
TUESDAY (JUNE)	27
WEDNESDAY (JUNE)	28
THURSDAY (JUNE)	29
FRIDAY (JUNE)	30
SATURDAY CANADA DAY (CAN)	1
SUNDAY	2

July 2023

MONDAY ○   3

TUESDAY INDEPENDENCE DAY (US)   4

WEDNESDAY   5

THURSDAY   6

FRIDAY 7

SATURDAY 8

SUNDAY 9

My power is already within.

July 2023

MONDAY ☽

10

TUESDAY

11

WEDNESDAY

12

THURSDAY

13

FRIDAY 14

SATURDAY 15

SUNDAY 16

I am ready to see things in a new light.

July 2023

MONDAY ● 17

TUESDAY 18

WEDNESDAY 19

THURSDAY 20

FRIDAY

21

SATURDAY

22

SUNDAY

23

I am divinely guided toward my destiny.

July 2023

MONDAY

24

TUESDAY

25

WEDNESDAY

26

THURSDAY

27

FRIDAY

28

SATURDAY

29

SUNDAY

30

*The answers
I need
are already
inside of me.*

My energy creates
my reality. I am ready
and willing to use this power
with intention and for good.

MOST POWERFUL YOU

All energy is interconnected, both here on planet Earth and in the Universe. What does this mean? It means you are one with the Universe. You are more powerful than you know! One rule is constant: the energy you put out is the energy you receive back. What shows up in your physical reality is a direct reflection of the energy you are giving off through your thoughts, feelings, and vibration.

Think about how you've been showing up in life.

- Do you generally look at the bright side of things or are you always complaining?
- Are you kind and generous to others or do you think everyone is out to get you?
- Are you excited about the future or always worrying about it?

These questions can give you clues as to why certain scenarios keep playing out in your life.

August 2023

NOTES	SUNDAY	MONDAY	TUESDAY
			○ 1
	6	7 ☽	8
		SUMMER BANK HOLIDAY (UK-SCT)	
	13	14	15
	20	21	22
	27	28	29
		SUMMER BANK HOLIDAY (UK-ENG / NIR / WAL)	

August 2023

WEDNESDAY	THURSDAY	FRIDAY	SATURDAY
2	3	4	5
9	10	11	12
● 16	17	18	19
23 ☾	24	25	26
○ 30	31		

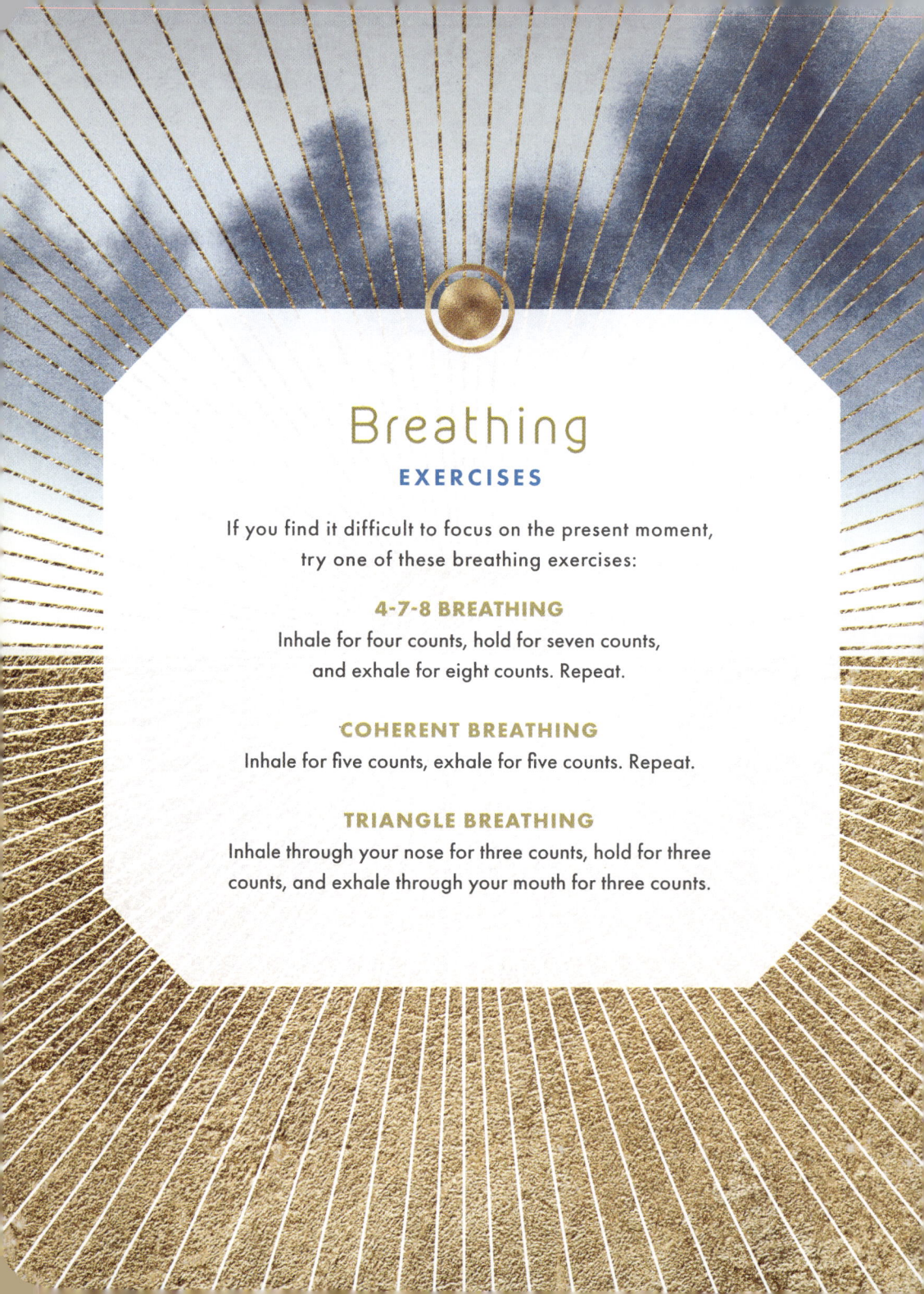

Breathing

EXERCISES

If you find it difficult to focus on the present moment,
try one of these breathing exercises:

4-7-8 BREATHING

Inhale for four counts, hold for seven counts,
and exhale for eight counts. Repeat.

COHERENT BREATHING

Inhale for five counts, exhale for five counts. Repeat.

TRIANGLE BREATHING

Inhale through your nose for three counts, hold for three
counts, and exhale through your mouth for three counts.

July/August

MONDAY (JULY)   31

TUESDAY ○   1

WEDNESDAY   2

THURSDAY   3

FRIDAY   4

SATURDAY   5

SUNDAY   6

August 2023

MONDAY SUMMER BANK HOLIDAY (UK-SCT)

7

TUESDAY 🌙

8

WEDNESDAY

9

THURSDAY

10

FRIDAY 11

SATURDAY 12

SUNDAY 13

My energy creates my reality.

August 2023

MONDAY   14

TUESDAY   15

WEDNESDAY ●   16

THURSDAY   17

FRIDAY 18

SATURDAY 19

SUNDAY 20

I have
the power
to create
my life.

August 2023

MONDAY 21

TUESDAY 22

WEDNESDAY 23

THURSDAY ◖ 24

FRIDAY 25

SATURDAY 26

SUNDAY 27

It's easy for me to achieve my goals.

SEPTEMBER

I manifest my dreams
effortlessly.

MANIFESTATION

Your feelings are your inner guidance system. Think of them as feedback from the Universe. They are letting you know whether or not you are on the right track. When in doubt, focus on what feels good and you will shift your vibration. There are two types of manifesting: manifesting from your ego and manifesting from your higher self.

Manifesting from Your Ego

When you are manifesting from your ego, you are manifesting what you think will make you happy. Oftentimes, this is something that looks great on the outside, but lacks substance and isn't what will make you happy in the long run. This also may be what our brain tells us is reasonable. These questions can give you clues as to why certain scenarios keep playing out in your life.

Manifesting from Your Higher Self

When you are manifesting from your higher self, you are manifesting what will truly make you happy.

September 2023

NOTES	SUNDAY	MONDAY	TUESDAY
	3	4	5
	FATHER'S DAY (AUS / NZ) 10	LABOR DAY (US) LABOUR DAY (CAN) 11	12
	GRANDPARENTS' DAY (US) 17	PATRIOT DAY (US) 18	19
	24	25	26
	YOM KIPPUR (BEGINS AT SUNDOWN)		

September 2023

WEDNESDAY	THURSDAY	FRIDAY	SATURDAY
		1	2
☽ 6	7	8	9
13 ●	14	15	16
		ROSH HASHANAH (BEGINS AT SUNDOWN) **FIRST DAY OF NATIONAL HISPANIC HERITAGE MONTH**	
20	21 ◑	22	23
			FALL EQUINOX
27	28 ○	29	30
		SUKKOT (BEGINS AT SUNDOWN)	

Visualize

YOUR DREAM DAY

Look at your entire life as a whole, then visualize what your
dream day looks like. Consider:

*If you had all the money in the world,
what would your day look like?*

• • •

Who would be with you? Where would you live?

• • •

What would you do for fun?

• • •

What would be your purpose?

All these areas of your life are interconnected and all affect
one another. Try to see the big picture—the grand vision.

August/September

MONDAY (AUGUST) SUMMER BANK HOLIDAY (UK-ENG / NIR / WAL)   28

TUESDAY (AUGUST)   29

WEDNESDAY (AUGUST) ○   30

THURSDAY (AUGUST)   31

FRIDAY   1

SATURDAY   2

SUNDAY FATHER'S DAY (AUS / NZ)   3

September 2023

MONDAY LABOR DAY (US) / LABOUR DAY (CAN)

4

TUESDAY

5

WEDNESDAY ◗

6

THURSDAY

7

FRIDAY 8

SATURDAY 9

SUNDAY GRANDPARENTS' DAY (US) 10

Hold the vibration of love as often as possible.

September 2023

MONDAY PATRIOT DAY (US)

11

TUESDAY

12

WEDNESDAY

13

THURSDAY ●

14

FRIDAY ROSH HASHANAH (BEGINS AT SUNDOWN) /
FIRST DAY OF NATIONAL HISPANIC HERITAGE MONTH   15

SATURDAY   16

SUNDAY   17

*Focus on
what you want
instead of
what you
don't want.*

September 2023

MONDAY 18

TUESDAY 19

WEDNESDAY 20

THURSDAY 21

FRIDAY ◖

22

SATURDAY FALL EQUINOX

23

SUNDAY YOM KIPPUR (BEGINS AT SUNDOWN)

24

I am filled with happiness and gratitude.

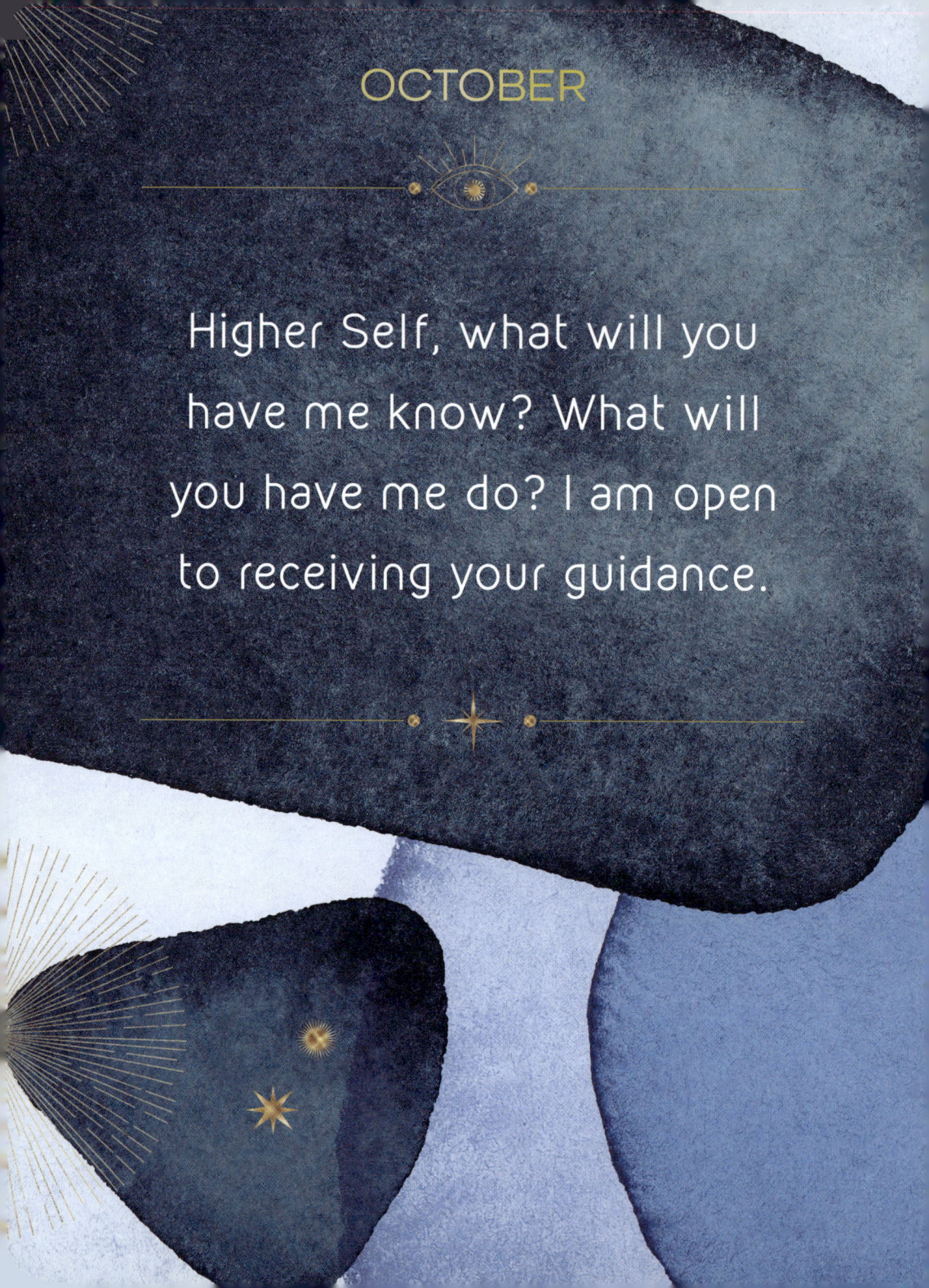

OCTOBER

Higher Self, what will you have me know? What will you have me do? I am open to receiving your guidance.

RECOGNIZE YOUR HIGHER SELF

Your higher self fully understands your oneness with the Universe. It knows that your manifestation has already happened. In fact, quantum physics tells us there are an infinite number of realities. We just have to align with the frequency of the reality we want. Where the ego only knows one way to get there, the higher self is able to align you with the path of greatest fulfillment. It is in a space of knowing it is already done. You just need to energetically align with it.

When you are manifesting from your higher self, you will have unwavering faith that your desires will manifest in the best possible way. We often try to control how things happen, but this is not needed. Your higher self always knows the best way to get you from point A to point B.

October 2023

NOTES	SUNDAY	MONDAY	TUESDAY
	1	2	3
		LABOUR DAY (AUS-ACT / NSW / SA)	
	8	9	10
		INDIGENOUS PEOPLES' DAY (US) COLUMBUS DAY (US) THANKSGIVING DAY (CAN)	
	15	16	17
	22	23	24
		LABOUR DAY (NZ)	
	29	30	31
			HALLOWEEN

October 2023

WEDNESDAY	THURSDAY	FRIDAY	SATURDAY
4	5 ☾	6	7
			SIMCHAT TORAH (BEGINS AT SUNDOWN)
11	12	13 ●	14
18	19	20 ☾	21
25	26	27 ○	28

Meditation

FOR CONNECTING WITH YOUR HIGHER SELF

1. First, create a sacred, relaxing environment where you feel safe and can easily calm your mind.

2. Next, sit down cross-legged or in a chair. If sitting on the ground, you can prop a pillow underneath you. Keep your back, neck, and head straight so you are a straight channel for energy to flow through you.

3. Now imagine a golden light coming down from the Universe through your Sahasrara, or crown chakra (top of the head), and traveling down your spine right into the Earth. This loving and healing light is going through you and wrapping around the Earth's core and flowing back up through you. This beautiful, pure light fills your entire being with every breath, and with each exhale, you release anything that is no longer serving you. You are now safely rooted and a clear channel for connecting with your higher self.

September/October

MONDAY (SEPTEMBER)   25

TUESDAY (SEPTEMBER)   26

WEDNESDAY (SEPTEMBER)   27

THURSDAY (SEPTEMBER)   28

FRIDAY (SEPTEMBER) SUKKOT (BEGINS AT SUNDOWN) ○   29

SATURDAY (SEPTEMBER)   30

SUNDAY   1

October 2023

2

TUESDAY

3

WEDNESDAY

4

THURSDAY

5

FRIDAY ☽   6

SATURDAY SIMCHAT TORAH (BEGINS AT SUNDOWN)   7

SUNDAY   8

Make gratitude a daily practice to stay connected with your higher self.

October 2023

MONDAY INDIGENOUS PEOPLES' DAY (US) / COLUMBUS DAY (US) / THANKSGIVING DAY (CAN)

9

TUESDAY

10

WEDNESDAY

11

THURSDAY

12

FRIDAY

13

SATURDAY ●

14

SUNDAY

15

Give gratitude for what you already have and for what you desire as though it's already yours.

October 2023

MONDAY 16

TUESDAY 17

WEDNESDAY 18

THURSDAY 19

FRIDAY 20

SATURDAY ☽ 21

SUNDAY 22

Miracles happen in my life all the time.

October 2023

MONDAY LABOUR DAY (NZ)   23

TUESDAY   24

WEDNESDAY   25

THURSDAY   26

FRIDAY   27

SATURDAY ○   28

SUNDAY   29

*I don't have
to be perfect.
I just need
to be me.*

NOVEMBER

I hold the wisdom
of the Universe
inside of me.

INTUITION vs EGO

Your intuition is your inner knowing. You can't explain it and it may not seem logical, but you have a strong feeling about something. Something excites you and lights you up even if it seems absurd to other people.

Doubt and limiting beliefs are the opposite. You feel uncertain. The ego will try to find the logic. If you find yourself questioning your intuition, know that this is your ego working really hard to keep the status quo. It is using your past experiences to create a possible scenario. Your intuition can see far past your limited experience. It sees all possibilities and will guide you toward the best possible outcome.

- To see how your intuition communicates with you, ask a question and ask for the answer within twenty-four hours.

- Pay attention! Your intuition can communicate subtly.

November 2023

NOTES	SUNDAY	MONDAY	TUESDAY
	5 ☽	6	7
			ELECTION DAY (US)
	12 ●	13	14
	FIRST DAY OF DIWALI		
	19 ☽	20	21
	26 ○	27	28

November 2023

WEDNESDAY	THURSDAY	FRIDAY	SATURDAY
1 ALL SAINTS' DAY	2	3	4
8	9	10	11 VETERANS DAY (US)
15	16	17	18
22	23 THANKSGIVING DAY (US)	24 NATIVE AMERICAN HERITAGE DAY (US)	25
29	30		

Meditation
TO OPEN YOUR THIRD EYE

The third eye is the gateway to heightened intuition. It is located just above and between the eyes. It's also known as the pineal gland, where the mind, body, and soul meet. It gathers information far beyond what your conscious mind can process.

This meditation will allow you to open your third eye and connect with your intuition.

1. Sit down and start taking a few deep breaths. Allow yourself to relax into the breath. If you feel anxious at all, keep focusing on the breath until you are in a state of relaxation.

2. Once you feel relaxed, bring your attention to the third eye region, up and between your eyes.

3. Imagine a beautiful golden light entering through your third eye. This is the gateway to your intuition. Visualize yourself stepping through this gateway into your desired reality.

Whenever you feel closed off from your intuition or second guessing it, you can do this meditation to reconnect.

October/November

MONDAY (OCTOBER)   30

TUESDAY (OCTOBER) HALLOWEEN   31

WEDNESDAY ALL SAINTS' DAY   1

5:00 Angela PRP - 95 -

THURSDAY   2

FRIDAY   3

9:00 Marleni Verrugas # 6 -
1:00 Miriam - 2do tratamiente.
6:00 - Olga - 10th

SATURDAY   4

Monica Hamit RF Caras Cuello

SUNDAY   5

November 2023

MONDAY 6

TUESDAY ELECTION DAY (US) 7

WEDNESDAY 8

THURSDAY 9

FRIDAY ~~Marlen F~~ - 9: -9:30. Verruga Fatante. **10**

2:00 - Mirian 3 er treatment -
~~Manet~~ -
6:00 Olya II tro treatmen Free -

SATURDAY VETERANS DAY (US) **11**

SUNDAY FIRST DAY OF DIWALI **12**

I let my
intuition guide
me down the
path toward my
highest good.

November 2023

MONDAY ●   13

TUESDAY   14

WEDNESDAY   15

THURSDAY   16

11:00 - Mirna

FRIDAY 17

SATURDAY 18

SUNDAY 19

My possibilities are endless.

November 2023

MONDAY ☾ **20**

TUESDAY **21**

WEDNESDAY **22**

THURSDAY THANKSGIVING DAY (US) **23**

FRIDAY NATIVE AMERICAN HERITAGE DAY (US) 24

SATURDAY 25

SUNDAY 26

*I am happy,
healthy,
and whole.*

DECEMBER

I intentionally
create my reality.

SET INTENTIONS
WITH PURPOSE

- What do you want this year?
- In five years?
- In ten years?
- When was the last time you've thought about it in detail?
- What was the last big life goal you set?

Sadly, there are so many people who have long given up on their hopes and dreams. They've thrown in the towel and settled for mediocrity in all areas of their life. They go through the days on autopilot. Those days quickly turn into months. The months quickly turn into years, and next thing they know, decades have passed.

You are in the driver's seat of your life, ready to take control and manifest your wildest dreams. It's never too late to chase your dreams, set a new goal, or change paths.

December 2023

NOTES	SUNDAY	MONDAY	TUESDAY
	3	4 ☽	5
	INTERNATIONAL DAY OF PERSONS WITH DISABILITIES		
	10	11 ●	12
	HUMAN RIGHTS DAY		
	17	18 ☾	19
	24	25 ○	26
	CHRISTMAS EVE		BOXING DAY (UK / CAN / AUS / NZ)
	31		
	NEW YEAR'S EVE	CHRISTMAS DAY	FIRST DAY OF KWANZAA

December 2023

WEDNESDAY	THURSDAY	FRIDAY	SATURDAY
		1 WORLD AIDS DAY	2
6	7	8	9
13	14 HANUKKAH (BEGINS AT SUNDOWN)	15	16
20	21	22	23
27	28 WINTER SOLSTICE	29	30

Reframe
YOUR GOALS

Often, instead of real goals, people tend to list the things they don't want:

I don't want to be in this soul-sucking job anymore.

• • •

I don't want a car that keeps breaking down.

• • •

I don't want friends that cause drama.

Remember, the Universe is always working, so don't give too much of your thoughts, feelings, and energy to the things you don't want. Instead, practice reframing those things into what you do want:

I want a job that brings me fulfillment.

• • •

I want a new, reliable car.

• • •

I want friends who are supportive and kind.

The good thing about being clear on what you will no longer tolerate is it helps you get really clear on what you are energetically available for. The next time you find your mind wandering to all the things that are no longer serving you, try reframing those things into new goals.

November/December

MONDAY (NOVEMBER) ○   27

TUESDAY (NOVEMBER)   28

WEDNESDAY (NOVEMBER)   29

THURSDAY (NOVEMBER)   30

FRIDAY WORLD AIDS DAY   1

SATURDAY   2

SUNDAY INTERNATIONAL DAY OF PERSONS WITH DISABILITIES   3

December 2023

MONDAY

4

TUESDAY ☽

5

WEDNESDAY

6

THURSDAY HANUKKAH (BEGINS AT SUNDOWN)

7

FRIDAY   8

SATURDAY   9

SUNDAY HUMAN RIGHTS DAY   10

I will act with intention today.

December 2023

MONDAY

11

TUESDAY ●

12

WEDNESDAY

13

THURSDAY

14

FRIDAY 15

SATURDAY 16

SUNDAY 17

There is a continuous flow of money into my life.

December 2023

18

19

20

21

FRIDAY 22

SATURDAY 23

SUNDAY CHRISTMAS EVE 24

*My life
is abundant
and full of
opportunity.*

December 2023

MONDAY CHRISTMAS DAY 25

TUESDAY BOXING DAY (UK / CAN / AUS / NZ) / FIRST DAY OF KWANZAA 26

WEDNESDAY 27

THURSDAY 28

FRIDAY   29

SATURDAY   30

SUNDAY NEW YEAR'S EVE   31

The Universe is responding to my thoughts and feelings.

JANUARY

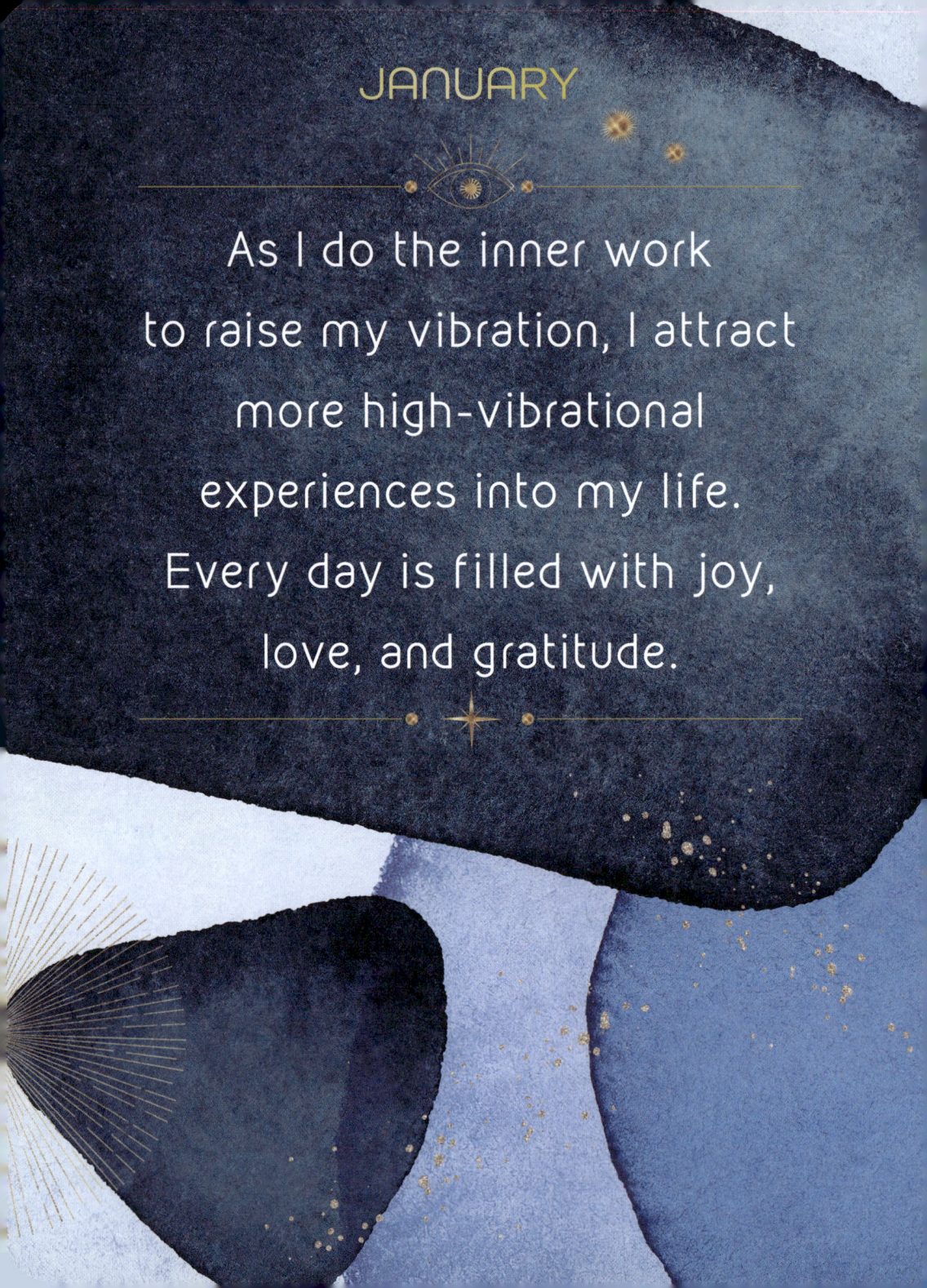

As I do the inner work to raise my vibration, I attract more high-vibrational experiences into my life. Every day is filled with joy, love, and gratitude.

POSITIVE PRACTICES TO RAISE YOUR VIBES

The following suggestions can help you tip the scales back to the positive when you feel your vibrational energies are low:

SMILING: Did you know that smiling releases feel-good hormones in your body? Even if it's forced, it still works. Smiling is also contagious. Test it out. Pick someone who looks like they're having a bad day and smile at them. I guarantee you'll get a smile back, and that one simple smile will probably change their entire day!

RANDOM ACTS OF KINDNESS: You will get just as much joy out of giving as receiving. Whether it's buying someone's lunch, holding the door open, or leaving money for someone to find, there are so many ways you can make a difference. These small acts have a ripple effect that extends far beyond what you can imagine.

LAUGHTER: As they say, laughter is the best medicine. You can't help but feel good after a good laugh. Watch a funny movie and allow yourself to lighten up. Don't sweat the small stuff. Instead, laugh it off.

January 2024

NOTES	SUNDAY	MONDAY	TUESDAY
		1	2
		NEW YEAR'S DAY	NEW YEAR HOLIDAY (UK-SCT)
	7	8	9
	14	15	16
		CIVIL RIGHTS DAY (US) MARTIN LUTHER KING JR. DAY (US)	
	21	22	23
	28	29	30

January 2024

WEDNESDAY	THURSDAY	FRIDAY	SATURDAY
☽ 3	4	5	6
10 ●	11	12	13
◔ 17	18	19	20
24 ○	25	26 AUSTRALIA DAY (AUS)	27 HOLOCAUST REMEMBRANCE DAY
31			

Make Manifestation

A HABIT

Our subconscious is controlling the show the majority of the time. This is why it's so hard to form new habits or quit old ones. Here are some practices that will help you integrate intentional manifestation into your daily life:

Question everything. This will help you bring awareness to your limiting beliefs and anything holding you back in your subconscious.

• • •

Check in with your thoughts and feelings throughout the day to see where your focus and energy are going. Hold the vision of what you want to manifest twice a day for two minutes.

• • •

Allow yourself to dream big and let your imagination run wild. Make gratitude a constant in your life.

• • •

Practice manifesting little things to build up your belief in the process.

• • •

Keep your vision front and center. Journal about it, create a vision board, and leave sticky notes or reminders with affirmations.

January

MONDAY NEW YEAR'S DAY
1

TUESDAY NEW YEAR HOLIDAY (UK-SCT)
2

WEDNESDAY ☽
3

THURSDAY
4

FRIDAY
5

SATURDAY
6

SUNDAY
7

January 2024

MONDAY

8

TUESDAY

9

WEDNESDAY

10

THURSDAY

11

FRIDAY 12

SATURDAY 13

SUNDAY 14

Today will be a positive day filled with joy.

January 2024

MONDAY CIVIL RIGHTS DAY (US) / MARTIN LUTHER KING JR. DAY (US) 15

TUESDAY 16

WEDNESDAY 17

THURSDAY 18

FRIDAY

19

SATURDAY

20

SUNDAY

21

I am
in a high
vibrational
state.

January 2024

MONDAY   22

TUESDAY   23

WEDNESDAY   24

THURSDAY ○   25

FRIDAY AUSTRALIA DAY (AUS)

26

SATURDAY HOLOCAUST REMEMBRANCE DAY

27

SUNDAY

28

*Everything
always
works out
for me.*

FEBRUARY

Feelings are just visitors,
and I can let them go.

DEALING WITH TOXIC ENERGY

I'm sure you can immediately think of at least one person who has toxic energy. This would be the person who leaves you feeling drained instead of energized. It's the person who is always complaining and looking at the negative in every situation. They may even put you down, make fun of you, or practice some form of mental or emotional abuse. It's easy to say you will simply cut this person out of your life. But what if this person is a family member, coworker, or longtime friend that you will inevitably see?

There are simple ways of dealing with toxic people:

- Keep things short, sweet, and surface level.
- Stick to topics that won't leave you feeling personally attacked.
- If the conversation turns negative, simply find a way to exit.

February 2024

NOTES	SUNDAY	MONDAY	TUESDAY
	4	5	6
			WAITANGI DAY OBSERVED (NZ)
	11	12	13
	18	19	20
		PRESIDENTS' DAY (US)	
	25	26	27

February 2024

WEDNESDAY	THURSDAY	FRIDAY	SATURDAY
	1 ☽	2	3
	FIRST DAY OF BLACK HISTORY MONTH	**GROUNDHOG DAY (US / CAN)**	
7	8 ●	9	10
			CHINESE NEW YEAR
14	15 ☾	16	17
VALENTINE'S DAY **ASH WEDNESDAY**			
21	22	23 ○	24
28	29		

Meditation

FOR SENDING LOVE

Love and gratitude are high-vibrational feelings. One of the most powerful things you can do to heal past hurts with toxic people is to send them love and gratitude.

Sit down with your back straight

and begin focusing on your breathing. No need to alter it. Just bring awareness to it. Now imagine a bright, golden light coming down from the Universe through your crown chakra and filling your body with this light, which is pure loving and healing energy.

Place your hands on your heart

and imagine this energy collecting into a big, powerful ball of light at your heart. You can take this ball and extend it outward to anyone. In doing this, you are sending them this powerful, healing, and loving energy. They may not realize it or understand it, but they can surely feel it.

This is an incredible way to send love and peace to anyone, including those you've had conflict with. It symbolizes you releasing them in a loving and peaceful way.

January/February

MONDAY (JANUARY)　　29

TUESDAY (JANUARY)　　30

WEDNESDAY (JANUARY)　　31

THURSDAY FIRST DAY OF BLACK HISTORY MONTH　　1

FRIDAY GROUNDHOG DAY (US / CAN) ◗　　2

SATURDAY　　3

SUNDAY　　4

February 2024

MONDAY 5

TUESDAY WAITANGI DAY OBSERVED (NZ) 6

WEDNESDAY 7

THURSDAY 8

FRIDAY ● 9

SATURDAY CHINESE NEW YEAR 10

SUNDAY 11

I forgive myself and others for any past hurts.

February 2024

MONDAY 12

TUESDAY 13

WEDNESDAY VALENTINE'S DAY / ASH WEDNESDAY 14

THURSDAY 15

FRIDAY ◗   16

SATURDAY   17

SUNDAY   18

I move forward with intention and clarity.

February 2024

MONDAY PRESIDENTS' DAY (US)

19

TUESDAY

20

WEDNESDAY

21

THURSDAY

22

FRIDAY   23

SATURDAY ○   24

SUNDAY   25

*I return often
to my natural
state of love.*

Today will be
a positive day
filled with joy.

START YOUR DAY RIGHT

Starting your day with enthusiasm and joy changes your entire outlook for the day, the work week, and eventually, your life as a whole. Set your alarm ten minutes early to focus on your wellbeing and watch how your days and mindset transform.

MOVEMENT: Start your morning by getting out of bed and doing five minutes of stretching and light yoga. Get the blood circulating to wake up your body. Movement helps you get out of your head and come into your heart. It moves the stagnant energy, so creative ideas can flow.

MEDITATION AND VISUALIZATION: Take at least two minutes every morning and evening to visualize your dream while feeling all the feelings of having it now. It's amazing how powerful this two-minute practice is.

GRATITUDE: Give gratitude every morning. Gratitude is at the center of manifesting. This is the easiest and fastest way to get in a high-vibrational state. If you want to attract more positive things in your life, you must be grateful for what you already have.

March 2024

NOTES	SUNDAY	MONDAY	TUESDAY
	☽ 3	4	5
	● 10	11	12
	RAMADAN (BEGINS AT SUNDOWN) MOTHERING SUNDAY (UK) ☾ 17	LABOUR DAY (AUS-VIC) 18	19
	ST. PATRICK'S DAY 24 ○	25	SPRING EQUINOX 26
	PALM SUNDAY 31 EASTER		

March 2024

WEDNESDAY	THURSDAY	FRIDAY	SATURDAY
		1	2
		FIRST DAY OF WOMEN'S HISTORY MONTH	
6	7	8	9
13	14	15	16
20	21	22	23
			PURIM (BEGINS AT SUNDOWN)
27 NOWRUZ	28	29	30
		GOOD FRIDAY	

Setting
YOUR INTENTION

Once you get crystal clear on what you want, it's time to set an intention and place your order with the Universe. When stating your desire to the Universe, firmly believe in putting pen to paper. Think of it as forging a contract with the Universe. It is declaring what you want. Putting it in ink makes it feel real and tells your mind to stop going back and forth. You've made your decision. This is what you want.

Dear Universe,
I am placing my order for (insert intention). I am open to receiving guidance in co-creating my reality. I have unwavering faith you will guide me on the path of least resistance. I fully trust the process and surrender control. Thank you, thank you, thank you!

February/March

MONDAY (FEBRUARY) 26

TUESDAY (FEBRUARY) 27

WEDNESDAY (FEBRUARY) 28

THURSDAY (FEBRUARY) 29

FRIDAY FIRST DAY OF WOMEN'S HISTORY MONTH 1

SATURDAY 2

SUNDAY ◗ 3

March 2024

4

5

6

7

FRIDAY   8

SATURDAY   9

SUNDAY RAMADAN (BEGINS AT SUNDOWN) / MOTHERING SUNDAY (UK) ●   10

*Awareness will
allow you to
adjust and
reframe anything
not serving your
highest good.*

March 2024

MONDAY LABOUR DAY (AUS-VIC)   11

TUESDAY   12

WEDNESDAY   13

THURSDAY   14

FRIDAY 15

SATURDAY 16

SUNDAY ST. PATRICK'S DAY 17

Practice bringing your awareness to what you're thinking, feeling, and doing.

March 2024

MONDAY 18

TUESDAY SPRING EQUINOX 19

WEDNESDAY NOWRUZ 20

THURSDAY 21

FRIDAY

22

SATURDAY PURIM (BEGINS AT SUNDOWN)

23

SUNDAY PALM SUNDAY

24

My actions create constant prosperity.

March 2024

MONDAY ◯   25

TUESDAY   26

WEDNESDAY   27

THURSDAY   28

FRIDAY GOOD FRIDAY 29

SATURDAY 30

SUNDAY EASTER 31

I am filled with joy.

APRIL

I am powerful
and limitless.

THERE ARE NO LIMITS

The only limits that exist are the limits your mind makes up. You get to set the boundaries of what is possible! Allow yourself to dream big. You're going to manifest anyway, so you might as well focus on manifesting the grandest version of your life.

The best way to visualize what you want is to put yourself in the scenario of actually having it. Go to places that represent your next-level goals. Get a room at a five-star hotel, purchase tickets to ride on a three-story yacht, or even just grab a drink at a high-end restaurant. The idea is to put yourself in the scenario of the next level you want to manifest.

Whatever it is that you want, give yourself the experience of having it:

- Walk through the model home.
- Try on the shoes.
- Window shop at designer stores.

April 2024

NOTES	SUNDAY	MONDAY	TUESDAY
		1 ☽	2
		APRIL FOOLS' DAY	
	7 ●	8	9
			EID AL-FITR (BEGINS AT SUNDOWN)
	14 ☾	15	16
	Elia B+X- 6 Monts. 21	22 ○	23
		PASSOVER (BEGINS AT SUNDOWN) EARTH DAY	
	28	29	30

April 2024

WEDNESDAY	THURSDAY	FRIDAY	SATURDAY
3	4	5	6
10	11	12	13
17	18	19	20
24 ADMINISTRATIVE PROFESSIONALS' DAY (US)	25 ANZAC DAY (AUS / NZ)	26	27

Unwavering Faith

EXERCISE

Unwavering faith means having faith long after it seems like it won't manifest. In order to fully believe it will manifest, you must first be absolutely convinced it is a possibility or you won't take the action needed to make it happen. You can do this by visualizing the outcome.

1. Close your eyes and imagine what you want has already happened and you're telling your friend how excited you are that it manifested.

2. Tell them about three obstacles you had to overcome to make it happen. By doing this, you are overcoming the limiting beliefs you hold around this desire.

This simple exercise will make your subconscious see the goal as already achieved, so it will no longer doubt whether or not it's possible, and the limiting beliefs will no longer matter. The subconscious doesn't know the difference between reality and fantasy, which is why this is so effective. By thinking you've already made something happen, your subconscious will stop trying to resist it and will now fully believe it's a probability for you.

April

MONDAY APRIL FOOLS' DAY

1

TUESDAY

2

WEDNESDAY

3

THURSDAY

4

FRIDAY

5

SATURDAY

6

SUNDAY

7

April 2024

MONDAY ●   8

TUESDAY EID AL-FITR (BEGINS AT SUNDOWN)   9

WEDNESDAY   10

THURSDAY   11

FRIDAY 12

SATURDAY 13

SUNDAY 14

Mine is a life that knows no limits.

April 2024

MONDAY 15

TUESDAY 16

WEDNESDAY 17

THURSDAY 18

FRIDAY   19

SATURDAY   20

SUNDAY   21

*I lead a life
I create
based on
my desires.*

April 2024

MONDAY PASSOVER (BEGINS AT SUNDOWN) / EARTH DAY
22

TUESDAY ◯
23

WEDNESDAY ADMINISTRATIVE PROFESSIONALS' DAY (US)
24

THURSDAY ANZAC DAY (AUS / NZ)
25

FRIDAY   26

SATURDAY   27

SUNDAY   28

Always talk about your desires in the past tense as though you already manifested them.

Love is my natural state.
I am tapped into the
frequency of love, and I give
and receive love freely. I love
myself unconditionally.

LOVE YOURSELF

Today, you are going to start accepting the real you. You will begin to love your so-called imperfections and realize they make you unique. You will start showing yourself the love and acceptance that society never gave you. This is where mirror work comes in. Mirror work feels really awkward at first but trust it is one of the most powerful things you can do to begin chipping away at the damage those moments did to your self-esteem.

- Go in the bathroom, lock the door so you can have privacy, and stand in front of the mirror, gaze into your eyes, and say "I love you" over and over again until you feel love wash over you and open your heart.
- List all the things you love about yourself. Show yourself the love and acceptance that you didn't get during those hard moments in your life.

When you feel good about yourself, you radiate positivity.

May 2024

NOTES	SUNDAY	MONDAY	TUESDAY
	5	**6** ●	**7**
	CINCO DE MAYO ORTHODOX EASTER	LABOUR DAY (AUS–QLD) EARLY MAY BANK HOLIDAY (UK)	
	12	**13**	**14**
	MOTHER'S DAY (US / CAN)		
	19	**20**	**21**
		VICTORIA DAY (CAN)	
	26	**27**	**28**
		SPRING BANK HOLIDAY (UK) MEMORIAL DAY (US)	

May 2024

WEDNESDAY	THURSDAY	FRIDAY	SATURDAY
☽ 1	2	3	4
FIRST DAY OF ASIAN AMERICAN AND PACIFIC ISLANDER HERITAGE MONTH			YOM HASHOAH (BEGINS AT SUNDOWN)
8	9	10	11
☾ 15	16	17	18
22 ○	23	24	25
29 ☽	30	31	

Write a Love Letter

TO YOURSELF

There are people that are waiting to see the real, authentic you. They need your gifts. The world doesn't need another carbon copy. The world needs to see the things that make you different. Embrace those things. Give love for all the things that make you different. Tell yourself about these things that make you unique and beautiful.

1. List all the qualities that make you unique.

2. What do people always compliment you on?

3. What things do people come to you for help with?

4. What are you proud of yourself for?

5. What have you had the power to overcome?

Write it all down! Don't be bashful. The only person that will see this is you, so let your heart go wild with all the wonderful things you embody!

MONDAY (APRIL) 29

TUESDAY (APRIL) 30

WEDNESDAY FIRST DAY OF ASIAN AMERICAN AND PACIFIC ISLANDER HERITAGE MONTH ◗ 1

THURSDAY 2

FRIDAY 3

SATURDAY YOM HASHOAH (BEGINS AT SUNDOWN) 4

SUNDAY CINCO DE MAYO / ORTHODOX EASTER 5

May 2024

MONDAY LABOUR DAY (AUS-QLD) / EARLY MAY BANK HOLIDAY (UK)   6

TUESDAY ●   7

WEDNESDAY   8

THURSDAY   9

FRIDAY 10

SATURDAY 11

SUNDAY MOTHER'S DAY (US / CAN) 12

I am healthy and strong.

May 2024

MONDAY 13

TUESDAY 14

WEDNESDAY ☽ 15

THURSDAY 16

FRIDAY   17

SATURDAY   18

SUNDAY   19

I am uniquely beautiful.

May 2024

MONDAY <small>VICTORIA DAY (CAN)</small>

20

TUESDAY

21

WEDNESDAY

22

THURSDAY ○

23

FRIDAY   24

SATURDAY   25

SUNDAY   26

*Abundance
is my
natural state.*

JUNE

I attract my desires
with ease.

QUANTUM MANIFESTING

One theory of quantum physics is that there is an infinite number of parallel realities right beside us in a different frequency. Just as you can switch the radio and tune into another channel, you can tune into different frequencies. This is done by embodying the feelings of having it now. Acting as if you have already obtained your desires and, most importantly, feeling the feelings of having them already is how this shift occurs. Your heart is the energetic conduit by which this is possible.

- Visualizing what you want while feeling it is activating brain-heart coherence. This manipulates the energy field that surrounds you, allowing for quantum manifesting to take place.

- Being in the present moment is the best way to quickly activate brain-heart coherence. A simple practice to bring your awareness to the present is to focus on your breathing.

- The easiest way to tap into the feelings of having your desires now is through gratitude. Give love and gratitude for it now as though it's already yours.

June 2024

NOTES	SUNDAY	MONDAY	TUESDAY
	2	3	4
	9	10	11
	16	17	18
	FATHER'S DAY (US / CAN / UK) 23	24	25
	30		

June 2024

WEDNESDAY	THURSDAY	FRIDAY	SATURDAY
			1 **FIRST DAY OF PRIDE MONTH**
5 ●	6	7	8
12	13 ☽	14	15
19	20 ○ **FLAG DAY (US)**	21	22
26 **JUNETEENTH (US)**	27 ☾ **SUMMER SOLSTICE**	28	29

Activating Heart Coherance

VISUALIZATION

When you come into a state of heart coherence, you are accessing powerful energy and using it to impress your desires on the electromagnetic field around you, aligning yourself to the frequency of manifesting your desires. Activating heart coherence requires immersing yourself in the present moment and looking within rather than focusing on the external environment.

- Begin by closing your eyes and placing your hand on your heart.

- Focus on your breathing and allow yourself to relax.

- Imagine a ball of light emanating from your heart and connecting with the light force around you.

- Visualize your desires as already manifested and tap into the feelings of love, joy, and gratitude.

- As you feel these heart-based feelings, see this light grow brighter.

- By embodying the emotions of that which you wish to manifest, that light force around you will match with the energetic state of those heart-centered emotions, causing a shift from one reality to another, also known as quantum manifesting.

May / June

MONDAY (MAY) SPRING BANK HOLIDAY (UK) / MEMORIAL DAY (US) 27

TUESDAY (MAY) 28

WEDNESDAY (MAY) 29

THURSDAY (MAY) ◗ 30

FRIDAY (MAY) 31

SATURDAY FIRST DAY OF PRIDE MONTH 1

SUNDAY 2

June 2024

MONDAY 3

TUESDAY 4

WEDNESDAY 5

THURSDAY 6

FRIDAY 7

SATURDAY 8

SUNDAY 9

My soul leads the way to my dreams.

June 2024

MONDAY 10

TUESDAY 11

WEDNESDAY 12

THURSDAY 13

FRIDAY FLAG DAY (US) ◗ **14**

SATURDAY **15**

SUNDAY FATHER'S DAY (US / CAN / UK) **16**

I am so grateful my desires are already on their way to me.

June 2024

MONDAY   17

TUESDAY   18

WEDNESDAY JUNETEENTH (US)   19

THURSDAY SUMMER SOLSTICE   20

FRIDAY ◯   21

SATURDAY   22

SUNDAY   23

My higher self comes from a place of pure love.

June 2024

MONDAY 24

TUESDAY 25

WEDNESDAY 26

THURSDAY 27

FRIDAY ◗

28

SATURDAY

29

SUNDAY

30

*Being open
to receiving
isn't selfish.*

JULY

My life is abundant
and full of opportunities

FINE IS NOT GREAT

So many are in a zombie-like state, simply going through the motions. They are on autopilot because they never questioned the path society laid out for them. They only looked outside for guidance rather than going inward. They tell themselves all kinds of excuses for why they don't feel fulfilled:

- Life is hard.
- Suck it up.
- I'm fine.
- This is the safe path. Anything else is scary and unknown, so I better stay put.

Fine is not great. Don't settle for a mediocre life just because someone told you it's the safe path. You weren't put here to simply exist. You were put here to live, learn, grow, and thrive! Are you thriving? Or are you existing?

If you are feeling restless or frustrated with your job, relationship, or life in general, it is because your higher self sees another more fulfilling path. This is when you need to pay attention. Listen to your intuition. The Universe is communicating with you and guiding you toward your purpose.

July 2024

NOTES	SUNDAY	MONDAY	TUESDAY
		1	2
		CANADA DAY (CAN)	
	7	8	9
	14	15	16
○	21	22	23
	28	29	30

July 2024

WEDNESDAY	THURSDAY	FRIDAY	SATURDAY
3	4 ●	5	6
	INDEPENDENCE DAY (US)		
10	11	12 ☽	13
17	18	19	20
24	25	26 ☾	27
31			

Journaling Prompts

WHAT LIGHTS YOU UP?

You may think you already know your life's purpose, but I challenge you to dig a little deeper and make sure you know why you want this. Have you chosen a particular path because it lights you up or is it simply a means to an end?

Here are some questions to ask yourself when you find yourself wanting something just because it's a means to an end. Write your answers down in your journal so you can reflect back on them and see the progress you're making.

What is the end result you're after?

• • •

If you knew you couldn't fail, what would you try?

• • •

If you knew you wouldn't be judged by others, what would you do?

• • •

If you had unlimited funds, what would you do?

July

MONDAY CANADA DAY (CAN)

1

TUESDAY

2

WEDNESDAY

3

THURSDAY INDEPENDENCE DAY (US)

4

FRIDAY ●

5

SATURDAY

6

SUNDAY

7

July 2024

FRIDAY 12

SATURDAY 13

SUNDAY 14

My dreams
are bigger than
my fears.

July 2024

MONDAY

15

TUESDAY

16

WEDNESDAY

17

THURSDAY

18

FRIDAY   19

SATURDAY   20

SUNDAY ○   21

*The world needs
what I have
to offer.*

July 2024

MONDAY   22

TUESDAY   23

WEDNESDAY   24

THURSDAY   25

FRIDAY

26

SATURDAY 🌓

27

SUNDAY

28

Taking action will help you get out of your head and put your manifestation into motion.

AUGUST

I release fear
and open myself
to love.

INSPIRED ACTION

Most people doubt their intuition and just fantasize about taking action toward their dreams someday. Those fulfilling their purpose trust their intuition and take inspired action now. The best way to overcome your fears is by taking action.

Have you ever heard the saying "strike while the iron's hot"? This applies to manifesting as well. When you have an inspired idea, understand that it's coming through at that exact moment for a reason. The Universe has divine timing and is planting that seed of inspiration in you because it's the perfect time to take action. Oftentimes, we get inspired ideas and we tell ourselves we will come back to them later. The problem is, we almost never do. We completely forget about them. The more time that goes by, the more time our mind has to convince us it's a bad idea by coming up with all the ways it could go wrong and reaffirming all our limiting beliefs. Even if you do try to take action later, it's not going to have the same result, because you won't have the same creative energy flowing through you that you did the moment you received the idea. Trust the Universe and leap into action.

August 2024

NOTES   SUNDAY   MONDAY   TUESDAY

●   4   5   6

SUMMER BANK HOLIDAY
(UK-SCT)

11   12   13

18 ○   19   20

25 ☽   26   27

SUMMER BANK HOLIDAY
(UK-ENG / NIR / WAL)

August 2024

WEDNESDAY	THURSDAY	FRIDAY	SATURDAY
	1	2	3
7	8	9	10
14	15	16	17
21	22	23	24
28	29	30	31

Protection

PRACTICE

When you feel paralyzed from taking action, start by redirecting the energy within. If you are ever overcome with fear and feel as though you need to be protected, this is a powerful practice to protect yourself and your loved ones.

- Find a quiet place where you won't be disturbed and sit in a comfortable position.

- Visualize a bright light coming down from the Universe and entering through your crown chakra.

- Feel the light collect at your heart and burst out of your heart, forming a protective bubble around you.

- Now extend this bubble around others as well.

- Repeat: *I am safe and protected. I am loved and supported. Everything will be okay.*

July / August

MONDAY (JULY)   29

TUESDAY (JULY)   30

WEDNESDAY (JULY)   31

THURSDAY   1

FRIDAY   2

SATURDAY   3

SUNDAY ●   4

August 2024

MONDAY SUMMER BANK HOLIDAY (UK-SCT)

5

TUESDAY

6

WEDNESDAY

7

THURSDAY

8

FRIDAY 9

SATURDAY 10

SUNDAY 11

I have unwavering faith that by holding my vision, all would be well.

August 2024

MONDAY 12

TUESDAY 13

WEDNESDAY 14

THURSDAY 15

FRIDAY   16

SATURDAY   17

SUNDAY   18

Things always seem to work out in my favor.

August 2024

19

20

21

22

FRIDAY

23

SATURDAY

24

SUNDAY

25

I rise above fear and take action.

SEPTEMBER

I am the creator
of my reality and I have
the power to manifest
my dreams.

RISE UP

We all have thresholds around what we will tolerate. We have thresholds around pain. We have thresholds around finances. We have thresholds around relationships. Once we dip below the lines we have set for ourselves, we either fall into despair or rise up and manifest better.

Ask for guidance: Many times, we reach our breaking point but feel hopeless. You know you want better but have no idea how to get there. In these times, guidance is always available to you. All you have to do is ask and listen.

Look for signs: If you feel stuck, you can also ask for a sign. Let the Universe know what your sign is. Pick a symbol that has meaning for you but is obscure enough that you don't see it on a regular basis. This way, when you do see it, you know it's the Universe giving you a sign to let you know you're on the right track and should keep moving forward.

Choose a different thought: Start with one thought and shift it to a slightly better outcome or another way. As you begin to choose a better scenario, thought, or feeling, you can slowly begin to climb out of the hole of despair and into the realm of hope.

September 2024

NOTES	SUNDAY	MONDAY	TUESDAY
		1 ●	2	3
	FATHER'S DAY (AUS / NZ)	**LABOR DAY (US)** **LABOUR DAY (CAN)**	
	8	9	10
	GRANDPARENTS' DAY (US)		
	15	16 ○	17
	FIRST DAY OF NATIONAL HISPANIC HERITAGE MONTH		
	22	23 ◗	24
	FALL EQUINOX		
	29	30	

September 2024

WEDNESDAY	THURSDAY	FRIDAY	SATURDAY
4	5	6	7
11	12	13	14
PATRIOT DAY (US) 18	19	20	21
25	26	27	28

Manifesting
MINI STEPS

When you're trying to manifest something really big and it doesn't happen right away, it's easy to lose hope. This happens a lot with people who are brand new to the manifestation process. Their desire doesn't come to fruition right away or in the way they thought it would, and they say manifesting doesn't work.

Give yourself a small win. Maybe your big goal is to be a millionaire, but you can't even fathom what it would be like to be a millionaire. It's such a big goal compared to where you are that you don't truly believe it's possible. It can leave you feeling hopeless. If this is the case, give yourself a small win. Start with manifesting $100. Then once that happens, you try manifesting $1,000. Keep building your manifesting muscle, and your confidence and belief will follow. As you see proof of manifestation show up time and time again, your big dream of being a millionaire all of the sudden seems believable, and your hope is restored.

August/September

MONDAY (AUGUST) SUMMER BANK HOLIDAY (UK-ENG / NIR / WAL) ◗

26

TUESDAY (AUGUST)

27

WEDNESDAY (AUGUST)

28

THURSDAY (AUGUST)

29

FRIDAY (AUGUST)

30

SATURDAY (AUGUST)

31

SUNDAY FATHER'S DAY (AUS / NZ)

1

September 2024

MONDAY LABOR DAY (US) / LABOUR DAY (CAN) ● 2

TUESDAY 3

WEDNESDAY 4

THURSDAY 5

FRIDAY 6

SATURDAY 7

SUNDAY GRANDPARENTS' DAY (US) 8

When manifesting, start small and work your way up to bigger things.

September 2024

MONDAY   9

TUESDAY   10

WEDNESDAY PATRIOT DAY (US) ◖   11

THURSDAY   12

FRIDAY

13

SATURDAY

14

SUNDAY FIRST DAY OF NATIONAL HISPANIC HERITAGE MONTH

15

Nourish your mind with as many good thoughts and feelings as you can.

September 2024

MONDAY 16

TUESDAY ○ 17

WEDNESDAY 18

THURSDAY 19

FRIDAY   20

SATURDAY   21

SUNDAY FALL EQUINOX   22

I attract money through love and joy.

September 2024

MONDAY

23

TUESDAY

24

WEDNESDAY

25

THURSDAY

26

FRIDAY

27

SATURDAY

28

SUNDAY

29

I attract my desires with ease.

OCTOBER

I breathe in calmness
and strength.

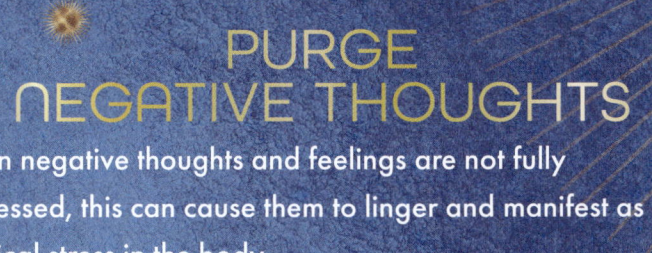

PURGE
NEGATIVE THOUGHTS

When negative thoughts and feelings are not fully expressed, this can cause them to linger and manifest as physical stress in the body.

- A helpful technique for ridding yourself of these feelings is to do a journal rampage, where you write out everything that is stressing you out that you wish to release. A lot of emotions can arise from this exercise, so find a space where you feel free to openly release these emotions. Don't hold back. Let it all out. No one will see it, so allow yourself to freely express anything that comes through. This is a great time to also release any judgment or limiting beliefs that are not serving you.

- When you are finished, rip up the paper and throw it out or burn it, symbolizing your release of these suppressed feelings and experiences. This may become a ritual you perform once a month during the full moon, as the energy of the full moon can cause many things to rise to the surface and stir up emotions.

October 2024

NOTES	SUNDAY	MONDAY	TUESDAY
			1
	6	7	8
		LABOUR DAY (AUS-ACT / NSW / SA)	
	13	14	15
		INDIGENOUS PEOPLES' DAY (US) COLUMBUS DAY (US) THANKSGIVING DAY (CAN)	
	20	21	22
	27	28	29
		LABOUR DAY (NZ)	

October 2024

WEDNESDAY	THURSDAY	FRIDAY	SATURDAY
● 2	3	4	5
ROSH HASHANAH (BEGINS AT SUNDOWN)			
9	◐ 10	11	12
		YOM KIPPUR (BEGINS AT SUNDOWN)	
16	○ 17	18	19
SUKKOT (BEGINS AT SUNDOWN)			
23	◑ 24	25	26
	SIMCHAT TORAH (BEGINS AT SUNDOWN)		
30	31		
	FIRST DAY OF DIWALI HALLOWEEN		

Meditation
EMOTIONAL DETOX

We are programmed to feel shame around expressing emotions like anger, rage, or sadness. Guilt, shame, frustration, and resentment can manifest in the body as tension, aches, and stiffness. One way to clear this energy is with a body scan meditation.

1. Start by sitting down with your feet planted on the ground and your back straight.

2. Begin scanning your body, starting with the top of your head all the way down to the soles of your feet.

3. Notice any tension, aches, pains, or stiffness in the body and breathe deeply into those areas.

4. With each breath, imagine creating space in those areas in between all of your cells.

5. Feel the peace wash over you as you continue this practice throughout your entire body.

September/October

MONDAY (SEPTEMBER) 30

TUESDAY 1

WEDNESDAY ROSH HASHANAH (BEGINS AT SUNDOWN) ● 2

THURSDAY 3

FRIDAY 4

SATURDAY 5

SUNDAY 6

October 2024

MONDAY LABOUR DAY (AUS-ACT / NSW / SA)

7

TUESDAY

8

WEDNESDAY

9

THURSDAY ●

10

FRIDAY YOM KIPPUR (BEGINS AT SUNDOWN) 11

SATURDAY 12

SUNDAY 13

When letting go of things, feel gratitude for lessons they taught you.

October 2024

MONDAY INDIGENOUS PEOPLES' DAY (US) / COLUMBUS DAY (US) / THANKSGIVING DAY (CAN)　14

TUESDAY　15

WEDNESDAY SUKKOT (BEGINS AT SUNDOWN)　16

THURSDAY ○　17

FRIDAY

18

SATURDAY

19

SUNDAY

20

Be the energy you wish to attract.

October 2024

MONDAY   21

TUESDAY   22

WEDNESDAY   23

THURSDAY SIMCHAT TORAH (BEGINS AT SUNDOWN) ◗   24

GET IN A FLOW STATE

Have you ever deeply submerged yourself into a creative project where hours went by and it felt like minutes? You were in a state of creative flow, living in the present moment. When you are living in the present moment, you activate brain-heart coherence. It's in this state that you can use the energy in your heart to impress your desires on the energetic field around you, beginning the manifestation process.

As you immerse yourself in the creative process and tap into that flow state, you become a clear, open channel with the Universe, which allows you to receive inspired ideas and wisdom. There are so many ways to get creative, whether it's coloring, painting, knitting, cooking a new dish, or anything else that brings your attention to the creative process.

We are all creative beings and tapping into your true creative nature will awaken you to a world of possibility.

November 2024

NOTES	SUNDAY	MONDAY	TUESDAY
	3	4	5
			ELECTION DAY (US)
	10	11	12
		VETERANS DAY (US)	
	17	18	19
	24	25	26

November 2024

WEDNESDAY	THURSDAY	FRIDAY	SATURDAY
		● 1	2
		ALL SAINTS' DAY	
6	7	8 ◗	9
13	14 ○	15	16
20	21 ◗	22	23
27	28	29	30
	THANKSGIVING DAY (US)	NATIVE AMERICAN HERITAGE DAY (US)	

Journaling Prompts

FIND YOUR SPARK

When was the last time you had a deep belly laugh? When was the last time you got lost in the moment and forgot about time? Instead of being so serious, wouldn't it be fun to let your imagination run wild? Wouldn't it feel refreshing to dream big? Wouldn't it feel good to wake up filled with joy?

It's time to find your creative spark and get in touch with that childlike imagination once again. Here are some journal prompts to help your imagination break free and run wild:

If you knew you wouldn't be judged, what would you do? How would you be? What path would you pursue? What would you stop doing?

• • •

If you knew you couldn't fail, what would you do? How would you be? What path would you pursue?

• • •

If you had a billion dollars, what would you do today?

• • •

What is something creative you enjoyed doing as a child?

October/November

MONDAY (OCTOBER) LABOUR DAY (NZ)

28

TUESDAY (OCTOBER)

29

WEDNESDAY (OCTOBER)

30

THURSDAY (OCTOBER) FIRST DAY OF DIWALI / HALLOWEEN

31

FRIDAY ALL SAINTS' DAY ●

1

SATURDAY

2

SUNDAY

3

November 2024

MONDAY 4

TUESDAY ELECTION DAY (US) 5

WEDNESDAY 6

THURSDAY 7

FRIDAY

8

SATURDAY ◖

9

SUNDAY

10

You are never too old to use your imagination.

November 2024

MONDAY VETERANS DAY (US)　　　　　　　　　　　11

TUESDAY　　　　　　　　　　　12

WEDNESDAY　　　　　　　　　　　13

THURSDAY　　　　　　　　　　　14

FRIDAY ○   15

SATURDAY   16

SUNDAY   17

Dream big and start something new.

November 2024

MONDAY 18

TUESDAY 19

WEDNESDAY 20

THURSDAY 21

FRIDAY ☽   22

SATURDAY   23

SUNDAY   24

I choose to be happy right now.

DECEMBER

Joy, love, and abundance
are my natural state.

YOU CAN'T MESS THIS UP

You literally cannot mess this up! Life is a game. The goal is not perfection. The goal is to continually learn, grow, and experience what you are meant to in this lifetime. You are human. You will make mistakes. Sometimes those mistakes will be the result of letting your ego guide you instead of your higher self. Other times, those mistakes are actually blessings in disguise. It could very well be the Universe throwing a wrench in your plan to steer you toward a better path. As you grow, keep in mind:

- When you find yourself in these situations where past limiting beliefs are holding you back or you fall back into a negative mindset, give yourself grace. This is not a one and done. It is a lifelong journey of learning and growing.

- No matter what comes up in your external environment, you always have control. It is within you that you create your reality, and that is where you will always find the answers you're seeking.

- It's important to trust your feelings, intuition, higher self, and most of all, the Universe. You have the wisdom of the entire Universe within you. You can tap into it whenever you need to. Never forget how powerful you truly are.

December 2024

NOTES	SUNDAY	MONDAY	TUESDAY
	● 1	2	3
	WORLD AIDS DAY		INTERNATIONAL DAY OF PERSONS WITH DISABILITIES
	◑ 8	9	10
			HUMAN RIGHTS DAY
	○ 15	16	17
	◗ 22	23	24
			CHRISTMAS EVE
	29 ● 30		31
			NEW YEAR'S EVE

December 2024

WEDNESDAY	THURSDAY	FRIDAY	SATURDAY
4	5	6	7
11	12	13	14
18	19	20	21 WINTER SOLSTICE
25 CHRISTMAS DAY HANUKKAH (BEGINS AT SUNDOWN)	26 BOXING DAY (UK / CAN / AUS / NZ) FIRST DAY OF KWANZAA	27	28

Anchoring
WITH SCENTS AND MUSIC

Here you will learn how to pair a new scent or song with a high-vibrational state. After doing so, the song or scent will serve as a trigger to instantly put you in a high-vibrational state. Recall a strong, beneficial emotional state. See what you saw, feel what you felt, hear what you heard. Relive the experience in your mind.

- Choose your anchor by selecting a scent or a song that you like.

- Meditate with your anchor.

- Once you are in that high-vibrational state, hold those feelings with the anchor for a few seconds.

- Break the state by engaging your brain. Do a math equation, ask yourself a strange question, or do something else to break you out of the high-vibe state.

- Repeat the previous three steps several times.

- After repeating, test this out by using the anchor to see if it triggers that high-vibrational state. If it does, you have established a strong anchor that you can now use anytime to get yourself instantly in a high-vibrational state.

November/December

MONDAY (NOVEMBER)	25
TUESDAY (NOVEMBER)	26
WEDNESDAY (NOVEMBER)	27
THURSDAY (NOVEMBER) THANKSGIVING DAY (US)	28
FRIDAY (NOVEMBER) NATIVE AMERICAN HERITAGE DAY (US)	29
SATURDAY (NOVEMBER)	30
SUNDAY WORLD AIDS DAY ●	1

December 2024

MONDAY 2

TUESDAY INTERNATIONAL DAY OF PERSONS WITH DISABILITIES 3

WEDNESDAY 4

THURSDAY 5

FRIDAY

6

SATURDAY

7

SUNDAY ◖

8

I am consciously creating my future.

December 2024

MONDAY

9

TUESDAY HUMAN RIGHTS DAY

10

WEDNESDAY

11

THURSDAY

12

FRIDAY

13

SATURDAY

14

SUNDAY ○

15

I have the ability to choose new thoughts and beliefs that help me manifest a better life.

December 2024

MONDAY 16

TUESDAY 17

WEDNESDAY 18

THURSDAY 19

FRIDAY

20

SATURDAY WINTER SOLSTICE

21

SUNDAY ☽

22

I am filled with wellness and vitality.

December 2024

MONDAY   23

TUESDAY CHRISTMAS EVE   24

WEDNESDAY CHRISTMAS DAY / HANUKKAH (BEGINS AT SUNDOWN)   25

THURSDAY BOXING DAY (UK / CAN / AUS / NZ) / FIRST DAY OF KWANZAA   26

FRIDAY 27

SATURDAY 28

SUNDAY 29

I am divinely guided toward my destiny.

December 2024

MONDAY ● 30

TUESDAY NEW YEAR'S EVE 31

WEDNESDAY (JANUARY) NEW YEAR'S DAY 1

THURSDAY (JANUARY) 2

NOTES

NOTES

....

....

....

....

....

....

....

....

....

....

....

....

....

....

....

....

....

....

....

....

NOTES

NOTES